THE
WHISPERING
GALLERY

ALSO BY WILLIAM LOGAN

poetry

SAD-FACED MEN (1982)
DIFFICULTY (1985)
SULLEN WEEDY LAKES (1988)
VAIN EMPIRES (1998)
NIGHT BATTLE (1999)
MACBETH IN VENICE (2003)

criticism

ALL THE RAGE (1998)
REPUTATIONS OF THE TONGUE (1999)
DESPERATE MEASURES (2002)
THE UNDISCOVERED COUNTRY (2005)

THE
WHISPERING
GALLERY

WILLIAM

LOGAN

PENGUIN POETS

PENGUIN BOOKS

Published by the Penguin Group
Penguin Group (USA) Inc., 375 Hudson Street, New York, New York 10014, U.S.A.
Penguin Group (Canada), 90 Eglinton Avenue East, Suite 700, Toronto, Ontario, Canada M4P 2Y3
(a division of Pearson Penguin Canada Inc.)
Penguin Books Ltd, 80 Strand, London WC2R 0RL, England
Penguin Ireland, 25 St Stephen's Green, Dublin 2, Ireland (a division of Penguin Books Ltd)
Penguin Group (Australia), 250 Camberwell Road, Camberwell, Victoria 3124, Australia
(a division of Pearson Australia Group Pty Ltd)
Penguin Books India Pvt Ltd, 11 Community Centre, Panchsheel Park, New Delhi - 110 017, India
Penguin Group (NZ), cnr Airborne and Rosedale Roads, Albany, Auckland 1310, New Zealand
(a division of Pearson New Zealand Ltd)
Penguin Books (South Africa) (Pty) Ltd, 24 Sturdee Avenue, Rosebank, Johannesburg 2196,
South Africa

Penguin Books Ltd, Registered Offices:
80 Strand, London WC2R 0RL, England

First published in Penguin Books 2005

10 9 8 7 6 5 4 3 2 1

LIBRARY OF CONGRESS CATALOGING IN PUBLICATION DATA

Logan, William,————
    The whispering gallery / William Logan.
        p. cm.
    ISBN 0-14-303617-3
    I.   Title.

PS3562.O449W48 2005
811'.54—dc22   2005043373

Printed in the United States of America
Set in Fairfield Light
Designed by Ginger Legato

for Julia Dowd

After ten years to discover
the confusion was untrue—
even now I'd do it over.
I'm glad the confusion was you.

CONTENTS

ACKNOWLEDGMENTS

Agni: Welcome to Paradise; *Columbia:* Jews; Nature; The Weather; *DoubleTake:* Lone Star i (as "Texas"); *Formalist:* To a Mirror; *Gettysburg Review:* Byzantium (Interlude); In the Swamp; Venice; Wren; *Hudson Review:* Lone Star ii (as "The Sea of Texas"); *Kenyon Review:* Eve; Lake; *Kunapipi:* Under the Palms; *Leviathan:* On the Acquisition of Pleasure in Small Groups; Song; *New Criterion:* Bank Voles at Trinity College, Cambridge; Deceit; The Devil's Toenail; Odalisque; The Old Burying Ground; An Ordinary Afternoon in New Haven; The River; Samphire; Swans; *New England Review:* Billy Budd; Coastal; Coup de grâce; Horseneck Beach Odalisque; Maple Leaves; *New Republic:* In the Museum (as "Ka"); *Notre Dame Review:* After the War; *Paris Review:* Endurance; *Parnassus:* Fermat; Therapy; *Partisan Review:* The Wax-Modelers; *Ploughshares:* After Easter; *Poetry:* Achilles; *Salmagundi:* Epitaph on an Editor; The Ides of May; The Ruins of Ostia Antica; Translation; *Sewanee Review:* Alphabet; Austen; Coleridge; In the Reign of Elizabeth II; Miss Lonelyhearts; *Shenandoah:* An Englishwoman in America; *Smartish Pace:* Crane among the Commoners; *Southern Review:* The Manatee; *Southwest Review:* The Dunes; *Times Literary Supplement:* The Prairie; The Real Thing; The Roman Villa; *Verse:* Ashbryn; *Yale Review:* Adultery; For a Fourteen-Year-Old Woman; Lying in Bed; The Rotting Stars; Seven Deadly Sin.

"Garbo," "Music Lessons," "The Past," and "Small Town" appeared in *Bright Pages: Yale Writers, 1701–2001,* ed. J. D. McClatchy (Yale University Press, 2001). "Prayer" appeared in *Words for Images: A Gallery of Poems,* ed. John Hollander (Yale University Press, 2001).

"If this ain't," said Mr. Peggotty, sitting down
among us by the fire, "the brightest night o' my life,
I'm a shellfish—biled too—and more I can't say."

—CHARLES DICKENS, *David Copperfield*

The whispering-gallery of the world . . .

—HERMAN MELVILLE, "Timoleon"

THE
WHISPERING
GALLERY

THE ROTTING STARS

I did not have the courage, that year,
to explore the nature of what I had seen.
A winter sun ignited the dry fronds,
but I sat at the prow of the old rowboat,

the cold river lapping hard rosettes
of barnacles along the rotting wharf.
They were like a drowned field of flowers.
The water eased in and out of the pilings.

Someone more sensitive might have heard it
as music. And vacantly, across the water,
came the tinny songs of an old radio.
The full moon lifted above the live oaks,

but just the crown, like a white dome out of Africa.
Meanwhile the sun had gone down.
The water turned cold dark, like speckled lead,
but the trees still held an eerie radiance

that lingers for a few minutes at sunset.
Just then a cormorant burst across the river,
its flight low and panicked.
It dove into the blackness and did not come up.

I knew then that my mother was dead.
Yet she wasn't dead.
She was living on the northern coast,
still the center of her bridge club,

still taking lunch each Tuesday at the marina.
I could see, in that empty, faded glow
even then leaving the river,
the irritated waves edged with silver tinfoil,

glinting, then a rich, dead India ink,
while across the waters, wavering at first,
came faint lanterns from the district houses,
like shrunken, unreachable stars—

I could see everything that was to come.

THE MANATEE

Beneath the ragged dock,
the cold gray water lapped
in miniature whitecaps
against the foreign rock.

The tidal, martyred St. Johns,
falling away at noon
toward an invisible moon,
glared like a breastplate of bronze

on some Renaissance soldier,
whose death's-head grin and spear
oxidized year by year
but never seemed to grow older.

I stood on weathered boards
the rusting nails had stained
like Dante's acid rain.
In the beginning was the word

and in the end the weeds—
floating, untied bows
stirring the gasoline rainbows
God's covenant guaranteed.

There, in the glassy glamour,
the oily reflected clouds,
floated a manatee, proud-
ly ignorant of grammar,

of the words not spoken,
her body a scarred moon
rising beneath the June
of surfaces unbroken.

Beneath the millennial roar
of Wall Street's stocks and bonds,
she gummed the milky fronds
along the gutted pier.

Beside her a round blue eye—
a baby manatee!—
like fresh philosophy
stared as new worlds passed by,

a leathery, magical Oberon
the waters arranged, then rearranged.
Next day the tide would change.
The baby would be gone.

TO A MIRROR

To know the words I say to you
are what I will betray in you
can only be to breathe in you
the darkness of the sea in you.

The image that will clear in you
will take me, but not near to you,
or say that if it dies in you
it chooses the Versailles in you.

It was a sin to lie to you
that time would ever sigh for you,
but one who has been lost in you
should know the permafrost in you.

No one who tried to stay in you
would ever know to pray for you.
The words I would evade in you
are lost in Everglades of you.

AN ENGLISHWOMAN IN AMERICA

NEW ORLEANS, 1858

Mrs. Sillery flirted with all the gentlemen
in true Southern fashion. I looked out the window
and saw pictures!—*immense* trees,
like oaks at Fontainebleau. I cannot believe

they are cypress. The star-shaped leaves
of the gum tree are red roses,
and the magnolia grows fifty feet high!
The way from the houses to the railroad

was made by planks from tree to tree.
Our American gentlemen wish *all* their widows
to marry in haste. Mrs. Sillery offered
to send some widows up from New Orleans—

I said I would send some from England
if they would give me an alligator. Said one,
"Oh, a thousand alligators for an English wife!"
Later, sailing down Prytania Street, I saw

a Brighton bathing-machine stranded there,
and over the door painted "Church of _____"
(I should have said,
"Church of the Mother of Bathing Machines"!,

but it was "Church of the DIVINE HUMANITY").
I was moved to see divine humanity, and found
myself in a room with fifty chairs and a pale preacher.
I saw some noble heads—a mulatto man

like a bust in the Vatican, marked Vespasian.
How I did burn to ask a few questions!,
but I came away as wise as I went, and very tired.
When I was in church, Mr. Sam Smith,

my distinguished relation, went up with a balloon
on the bare backs of two alligators eleven feet long,
at Place d'Armes (late Congo Square).
Yesterday, going to draw with my drawing hat,

I came upon six Negro children who ran away.
"Stop!" I said. "I do not eat niggers!"
They asked why I wore spectacles.
One, a little Topsy who sang and danced,

seized the youngest and screamed to me,
"I'll sell you this child for two dollars!"

THE DUNES

That year the sand dunes served our winter camp.
A figure rose in distance, the shattered blockhouse
arming the horseneck corner of the bay,
where currents fled the tormented sleep of harbor.

Bleached gulls tore holes in a sky of paper,
the Freudian gulls of troubled afternoons.
We lay in sand-couches, tolling secrets
with our backs to the land.

Our skin peeled away, and new skin peeled away.
That may have been precursor of fever.
On the horizon, the coasters hunted signs.
We decorated our thin legs with fish scales.

About that time, the wasting became general.
Later, standing in bus-station-green offices,
or corridors smelling of wet paint,
we waited for a town bureaucrat to sign

our documents, or countersign the scrawl
of other bureaucrats. The wait could go on for days.
The rooms were asleep, asleep with the scent of victory.
The same clerk might have signed the drowsy orders

for boxcars of salt to plough into Carthage.
No one demanded to see the documents again.
Later we were asked not to speak
the names of the children who died.

HORSENECK BEACH ODALISQUE

Gunmetal blue, then iris blue, then turquoise,
the plain of the Atlantic burned to steel
that summer along the Horseneck.
Our castles rose, dark and raggedly Gothic.
The dribbled turrets capped a moated wall,
and then the Muslim tide came roiling in
and took the holy cities one by one.
By August we were Moor-wasps,
each boy a white-toweled sultan of the waves.
Sand crabs scrabbled from our tightened palms,
burrowing downward through the pooling muck
to the icy realm of salt and shell. Each footprint
bred an archipelago. Across the boiling lagoon
of August, Martha's Vineyard reigned,
a bruised thumb above the feathery caps.
Mother was our harem, our peasantry.
Beside us a grand vizier on his crimson towel
(the New Bedford lawyer, his back a twisted hump)
sat patiently and watched the sunset come.

BILLY BUDD

Ivy poured from the chimneys like green smoke,
wind-whipped down the shingled roofs
that took forty years to rot, a season to discolor.
Sparrows lost themselves in the leaves—feathered gossips
who knew the dirty laundry of the town
and chorused dawn like a chain gang.
Boats docked each evening at the rotting wharf,
where boys balanced by the booms and floats,
gulls arcing, angling like old mariners,
now pleading, now flapping away in complaint.
Beneath the wooden bridge, pallid sponges grew.
Who knew what cursive secrets the water held?
Skunk cabbage swelled in half-light.
The gloomy black-and-white ghosts of television
promised to sear the world with new vision,
the fungal growth of the mushroom cloud.

I fought my battles with knotted ropes—
like Billy Budd,
shouting to my father, *Long live Captain Vere.*

ASHBRYN

The rocket-launches from Cape Canaveral,
vapor plumes rising on our little Magnavox,
nerved you to plunge your savings

into space-age metals.
If only you'd bought Polaroid or IBM.
What madness caught you up?

What madness did not?
We grew up to your get-rich schemes,
your blueprints for the "Tote-a-Boat"

you dragged one summer down Long Island beaches.
Our cellar was stocked with cases of miracle soap,
the soap that could devour all stains,

cost pennies to manufacture, was almost edible.
Aluminum was the magic word of our childhood.
After your holiday flight to go-go England,

you called it *aluminium.* You shipped home
a beef-red Morgan with a leather strap
and sat behind the wheel in your yachting cap.

It stands in dry-dock in your colonial garage,
its frame a weir of rot and hidden rust.
We always thought you secretly rich

behind your clouds of Lucky Strikes.
One year you were president of a yacht club,
but the balding manager flew to Rio

with a suitcase full of membership dues.
You set up again in real estate,
trading on that bewildered integrity

that bemused even your cautious creditors.
One by one we left the house on Private Road,
whose crooked, weeping chestnuts

spilled their spiked seedcases like harbor mines.
A summer's worth of paint peeled from the clapboards.
Oak stumps anchored the slanting lawn.

You sold Ashbryn the year before the market roared.

AFTER THE WAR

That was before the time I carried a gun.
The hearings ran for weeks, then months.
Through the rippled glass, my name
wrote a gilt verse in ancient Coptic.

Checked suits were all the rage that year,
but I cannot recall one newspaper headline
or who won the batting title.
One winter morning a woman broke

her heel in a sewer grating.
She stood on the sidewalk weeping,
clutching her red leather handbag.
She looked like my mother, or how I imagined

Mother had looked, twenty years before,
when she had come alone to New York.
The dresses of course were different then.
When young, she had lived in Philadelphia

in a house owned by gangsters.
Her father had been an oatmeal salesman,
and through the Depression they had never
lacked oatmeal or a Negro servant to stew it.

They were wary of Jews.
It might be true that they hated the Jews,
though they gave little thought to such people.
Would you mind getting me a napkin now?

My mother was a brunette in those days.
That was before we knew how many had died.
There were rumors—or rumors of rumors.
Had died in the camps, I mean.

I remember the smell from the basement carpet,
the black-and-white photographs
of mounds of homely horn-rims and gold watches,
the heavy ropes of human hair

sorted into their beautiful, inhuman colors.
By then it was much too late.
Long after the trials and the sentences,
my mother became a blonde.

UNDER THE PALMS

Behind the broken-knuckled palmetto,
face half-hidden, half-lit by razory fronds,
lost canvas of a Renaissance master
(lacking only the emerald glaze

of the parrot's outspread wing
or the dart and stitch of the hummingbird's
needlepoint), there you were, smiling and sexual,
skin aglow with new-world salt.

Behind you lay the cities of the plain.
The sky hung like a backdrop,
a foamy SOS-pad blue, darkening to storm.
You looked as if you could hear

the scuttle and whimper of undergrowth,
the downward exultation of roots,
the coral snake whose Magdalene beauty
(crimson sliced with black, like a Chanel suit)

could ravage whispers in the old tongue.
When I found you, face-down in a drawer,
fifteen years erased as if by the retoucher's art,
how young you were,

your beauty all in the varnish.

THE IDES OF MAY

Welcome, you high-pitched Antonies of heat!
The mortal cooling meat remains immortal
deep in the dying archive of the thistle.
Rapt, pincer-headed, feathers scaled like armor,
the quarreling turkey buzzards kneel to pray
furtively at their Caesar's decaying corpse.
Draped mournfully in black, they glisten with heat,
the squabbling senate of prairie undertakers
bewildered where the mock religious rite
for raising each new Lazarus goes wrong.
Conspirators beneath the lubber's whine,
slowly they flay the sinning from the skin,
as if the work were not what they enjoyed.
They flesh their beaks like new communicants.

FOR A FOURTEEN-YEAR-OLD WOMAN

Deep in your father's planted grove, the scrub
grew wicked. Bamboo stalks like Japanese screens
glittered with gold, as if laid leaf by leaf,
the way the wings of angels took their metal
inch on hard inch, in careless allegory.
So hours were told, so rich the hours told
until the Bible dream of innocence
was dreamed, rotting away. The live-oak branches
caught the last glint of sun, the light resentful
though on its way to absence, the oily dusk
settling like coal dust on the moss-hung boughs.
There, there within the tangled hair of shrub,
the coral snake coiled in silent invitation
to lay down the last burden of your childhood.

IN THE SWAMP

There lingered a disparity in the light
that gave the lake a brushed-over surface,
by which you meant, a trembling to the stillness,
as if the paint had dried even while flowing.
It was, you knew, absurd and yet, as a vision,
lacked nothing but the odor of decaying religion.
There we stood, after the drought of summer,
looking onto a dying lake at sunset.
Across its shallow reach, as shadows rose,
ibis came in lightly to roost, gliding over water oaks,
fluttering check-marks sinking along the glossy mirror,
then swerving at last into the dark cypress.
Each flight displaced the last, setting their beaks
like leather needles, their squawks spiraling
in the close din of argument. Each bird balanced
comically on a swaying twig. You could see
how nobly, how still, they tried to hold their heads.
In an hour, the bats would batter through darkness,
but not, not yet. There was time to watch
an alligator rise like an old man on all fours
on his miniature island
and make his way to the water, creakily,
as if roused from long sleep. And then the lake
took on that glint of tarnished silver-plate,
as if all that had happened were nothing,
as if what had yet to happen might be worse
than expected, or might never happen at all.

THE PRAIRIE

The flowers might have been named by children—
lantana, tickseed, pickerelweed, horned bladderwort.
Around us that morning lay the alligators,
the greenish brown of moldy suitcases, their eyes
heavy-lidded, as if they'd been kept awake all night.
A wood stork stalked the drying pools,
connoisseur of any flesh, as long as it was fish,
moving along the margins like a watchmaker
who had lost a tiny gear. The dry weeds ticked,
or tickled. It was late, late in the season,
as we passed the sinkhole, a green sea
of clotted hyacinth on which a bird might cross
from leaf to leaf and never drown.
We had been condemned to Paradise,
had stumbled down the sandy path
in our expensive clothes, one dawn
much like another, the gates unguarded,
the KEEP OUT signs removed. A fallen
palm lay discarded in the ditch, like a blunt sword
the departing cherubim had abandoned.
A drowsy river, more a canal than a river,
drained shyly into a culvert and disappeared.
The famous trees were gone, leaving scrubby bushes
that had no intention of growing any taller;
and in the distance herons posed, or sandhill cranes,
as if a painter had belatedly touched them in
with a bead of paint and a flick of the brush.
A gang of vultures, black as sin, tousled heads
sporting bad haircuts, loitered along the path,
waiting for the first heat to rise
so they could corkscrew into the sky.

The corpses on the prairie had nothing to do
but wait. The vultures shouldered each other aside
and, reluctantly, without a backward look,
beat their heavy wings into the sullied airs.
We knew then we could not be saved.

WELCOME TO PARADISE

"Welcome to Paradise," said the sign,
but the exit had flaked away. Everywhere rose the signs

of former wonders. No oranges
blossomed in the strip malls of Orange

City, Orange Mills, Orangedale, Orange Lake,
and the mirrored springs that fed local lakes

had turned snowy from the rural cement plant.
Even our outlandish tropical plants,

made to order the third day,
had to be imported, palms propped up Tuesday

on what Monday night had been an empty lot.
These days they think a lot about Lot,

the residents, hoping another real-estate boom
will swallow the half-built houses of the last boom.

They have forgotten the pillars of salt,
the mortal remains of Tristram and Iseult,

Abelard and Eloise. Love like regret
takes every anhinga Romeo, every egret

Juliet. Passed by rusting cars bearing bored
children, the gator on the peeling billboard

looks down on the roadside attractions and recommends
they stay shuttered for the winter that never ends.

COASTAL

We were headed toward the coast again,
the show of clapboards and shucked clams,
one spire pointed above the rooftops like a mast.
Out in the glassy gulf the masts slid by
like churches. Even the live oaks were Baptist.
The tomb of Christ was full of water,
and deep in the gulf the bones of apostles
laid reefs among the starfish,
each soul watching His deep-sea eye.
There was no room service in our motel,
just a clerk at the door with a Gideon,
asking over and over if we'd received the Word.
At dusk we staggered among the reeds,
scattering the fraught army of tiny crabs,
whisked back and forth in mute terror.
Fallen angels? Or risen devils?
Not that it mattered to the gods stalking them.
In the cemetery the bodies had been raised
above the water, the graves decorated
with shells. Our own bodies started at the end
and worked toward the beginning,
never sure how long death would give us.

LONE STAR

What do the blue hills night by night imagine
down in the ill-lit kingdom of the past?
They dream of being undersea again.

i.

You cupped the Indian paintbrush in your hand.
Here we were overlooked by passive steers—
shorthorns!—the local experts on the dust,
a dust made copper-green by spring's late rain.
Even the mesquite glowed, like marbled jade—
charred beyond life, alive where it couldn't be scraped
from tufts of virgin, or not so virgin, prairie.
I dreamt of nothings in the buzzing heat.
Above the wind-scoured fence posts and barbed wire,
electric poles just two generations old
marched up each country road where nothing happened.
Exhaustion contemplated the rusting barbs.
A roadrunner paused, then leapt the dreaming fence-wire.
The scissortail took up its listening post—
even the emptiness now has hush money.
The charity of strangers has worn down
each rocky-fingered outcrop stacked with fossils,
crumbling like a slab of Roman marble.
The lonely ranches have sprouted
satellite dishes, improbable blooms
that never turn blank faces to the light.

ii.

You walked across the dusty sea,
or what looked like a sea—raw, cracked,
the sea of doubt. The half-moon reared.
A ground-down, out-of-work mesa
had slumped beside it, sleeping or feigning sleep,
exhausted by the silence, the din of silence.
Spotted grasshoppers burred through drying weed.
A wire fence-line rode the mesa's back,
as if to say that it, too, had somewhere else to go—
and off it went. You were a vision,
shimmering down the lanes of prairie heat,
where late in spring the breeding crawfish swarmed.
Their skeletons lay bleached on the red crust,
like overturned hulls of tiny abandoned boats,
each oar a broken toothpick.
And there you were, closer, two steps closer,
taking your time, what time you had, strolling
across this dust bowl of a dried-up sea
whose Chinese glazes had opened up a crack
to the barren world below. When did you know
you never wanted a baby of your own?

AN ORDINARY AFTERNOON IN NEW HAVEN

It was Valentine's Day, a blind date,
and on the sidewalk, angry since I was late,

she sat astride the leather suitcase,
chain-smoking, frowning, wearing a lace

camisole, her blonde hair tied in a band.
I gave her my hand.

There followed the dizzy abbreviated spring
we were in love, flattering

our nervous unhardened animal
natures, knowing more the rise than fall

of love, or what we named love, having no better word.
Virgins are of course absurd,

say those who have forgotten the rest,
the French curve of a teenage breast

and all the destruction that follows, in bed.
Blossoms marked the spring of the dead,

the war stalled in the jungles of Vietnam,
the arrowy flights of SAM

missiles through the newspaper half-tone,
and, each night, her throaty voice on the phone.

Then she was gone, pregnant, to another life
from which she called years later, wife,

mother, unhappy in her tract house, wanting
something that could be no more than haunting.

What if we *had* exchanged rings,
bought station wagon, barbecue, a hundred things

for that life she knew the blueprint of
in the dull, resistant suburb of love?

How soon would I have packed to go?
I think of her sometimes. I don't know.

PENITENCE

i. Lake

April. Shadows crimson-edged, tattooed with light,
corrupt the visible in sweet intimacy.
Nature's backyard with ruined barbecue

falls toward the sinkhole lake, cricket frogs creaking
through the reeds, a brace of osprey suspended
overhead, whispery angels in the school of Tiepolo.

The lake turns a circle through Ptolemy's spheres,
nested one in another like Dante's *malebolgia*.
Decaying palm fronds rust at the edge

of dull water troubling the spattered half-sheen.
A turtle head breaks gray canvas
beneath the quizzical dependence of the dragonfly,

then bobs down to the habitation of souls.
The loyal angels modeled their fleshy bodies
on snapping turtles, never approached except at risk.

Subjugation arranges the soul,
each night the dark seeping in, roiling like a cloud bank,
then rim-shot thunder, a scrabble of lightning,

the drugged rush and release of tropical rain.

ii. The Past

Between the visible and invisible lies the alteration.
My father's skin turned hard at death,
no longer itself but the idea of itself.

He once took a scythe to an unkempt field,
the Platonic order lounging underground, secretive
as the mole burrowing until it reached the far lawns.

Raise us from our prostrate, inviolate forms,
O salt zephyrs peeling off the river, the river gone
in that form, that form only, in prayer or potency.

The past lies beneath our actions like a nail bed,
beneath the breeze's coil and frieze. Along the tide,
where sand crabs dug their quiet living,

the hillocks of the Vineyard arched and fell.
Sailors tore their catch from the billowing whale,
the barnacled cod, until the banks went dry,

abandoning the wind-scorched steeple like a rifle sight,
the graveyard tilting on its survey mark.
The froth of honeysuckle withered at the wall

as death built its sand-castle cities around us.

iii. Swans

C——, off-season. The old city mortared to new age.
Young men in flash suits own the footpaths.
Each railway viaduct to London frizzes with buddleia,

the "butterfly" bush, cocked refugee of empire,
amethyst spray whose roots drive home the cracks.
I was locked to the faith of another England,

shadowy walks up the weed-choked river,
a few out-of-work swans paddling to the bank
to hiss, or croak, or croak-hiss. Silence

drained the tributaries. The sculls and the boathouses
stammered in reflection, not themselves or quite themselves
on the water Canaletto made fetish of,

searing Venice into the seductive texture of oil,
then grinding scenes out, one after another,
until each cast its palsied shadow on the last.

I wandered spaded banks, mere ghost of myself,
still thirty and each brick arch bewitching to the eye.
Two godlike men laid Flemish bond in the aftermath.

The wall rose as the mortar fell.

iv. Deceit

Death never/always betrays retrospection.
Thou Shalt Not guards the approaches:
an asphalt road, a badly constructed hill, the view

laid out where patchwork fields sprawl in error.
Down through the medieval ridge and furrow,
summer lingers for the historical winter.

In a candlelit hall, the eighteenth-century sheep
offer their excuses and rise to depart;
the hero folds his cards and slinks away.

Who is not satisfied his superiors were mistaken,
that no one should feel guilty making a packet of money
or asking the shy girl to bed just once?

The eclipse comes round, late in the millennium.
The garden was rooted in understairs philosophy,
where each pig was equal to every other

and the cows were encouraged to form parliaments
and elect representatives who respected them.
No one can remain neutral when the age

catches us acting briefly, mistakenly human.

v. Music Lessons

Every Good Boy Deserves Favor. Again, *ritardando.*
Each Saturday the clubfoot teacher scored
posture and its struggling notes. Was it there

art learned its deceits? I sat in the car while scales
fell like distant, miniature empires, struggled to rise.
Finally my teary sister would emerge, piano books

spilling from her gabardine arms. Again, *forte.*
The cracked leather of Chevrolet was mine—
what immature Khan ever wanted more,

to hear the Abyssinian and still dream?
Sputnik's flawed arc stole night on night
through the doldrums of the Eisenhower years,

a brief sleep between nightmares under the cloudy aegis
of the H-bomb. The age demanded, not a question mark,
but ellipsis or the bang of explanation.

Our grace was to be permitted to live
where art, like the atom, embraced the eternal present,
notes pocking the surface of the finite

where *Eleven Greedy Boyars Demand Freedom.*

vi. Fermat

Fermat's Last Theorem. The will-o'-the-wisp,
might-have-been revolution starts with a name.
Newton made his calculus plot cannonball arcs,

and the Manhattan Project would have gone haywire
without a numbers man to hog-tie the formulas.
Poetry, not mathematics, offends the Divine,

but the Divine grabs weapons in both hands.
Fermat scribbled his conjecture in a margin
and lived thirty years judging obscure cases,

burning priests at the stake, never aspiring to the list
of geniuses killed in duels: Pushkin, Galois. How much
lost to women loved by men who were better shots?

Not many men have been moved by a calculation,
and the non-mathematical find even the simplest proof
less amorous than a bank statement. If not deceived,

Fermat took his secret to the coffin, trumped
centuries after by a local boy taking the wrong way
round the barn. Leibniz called the imaginary number

almost an amphibian between being and non-being.

vii. Samphire

Girls from the language schools go chittering
in birdlike tongues, small-breasted, doe-eyed—
Spanish or Italian, full of hormones, angst, vocabulary.

You caught me eyeing a Swede with bee-stung lips,
Botticelli face in a virgin's halo of blonde. Her breasts
spelled the old language through her cotton shirt.

A summer ago we stood ill in our bones,
unable to speak beneath the hail of argument
and never sure if our non-arguments survived.

Is *aphasia* the rain shower against speech,
burning in half-life longer than what surfaces?
I'm grateful for what you have chosen to ignore.

We discover again the cow paths worming our medieval city,
home farther than ever and myriad ways not to return.
In the market we buy tidal samphire, Shakespeare's

drenched vegetable, or Gloucester's, or Edgar's,
bulbous, green and salty, stripped hot with the teeth,
and not Shakespeare's after all, we learn by the book.

O vegetable love, a different vegetable entirely.

viii. *In the Reign of Elizabeth II*

How she loved her books going yellow,
cheap European paper taking acid in the face
and crumbling inside a lifetime, inside twenty years.

Why not go out of date, so much else was fixed
in the stingy socialism of five-year plans?
She knew she was going to live, by way of dying—

even the words couldn't hold life off forever:
the new coins thinned, rough-alloyed, one day
to be grubbed up by boys for whom Elizabeth II

would be distant as Roman emperors. The farms
still harrow their buttons of rust—soaked by nighthawks
in a jar of vinegar, out pour pocked visages

of a late Caesar, cast from turf-fired mints
with the country in slow-motion collapse.
The grandsons of Romans plighted themselves

to barbarians, each radiant, corrupting beauty,
twentieth-century eyes with a come-hither glance.
Our romances turn cold-blooded in memory

as the next millennium burns ours in offering.

ix. Eve

I never knew what you saw in yourself,
but you'd have given yourself lousy notices,
counting my ribs to see if one was missing.

The hot and bothered noons lure Cuban anoles
to the verge—black, bullet-eyed immigrants.
Our native patrician species, less seen every summer,

has taken to the trees, forsaken as gods. What changes
changes so slowly not even memory can be precise.
The past comes round like a salesman again—

who would have thought the roads would be full
of Volkswagens, their third great age!
Commerce has its converts: our mail shuttles

through the Satanic mills of the telephone. We're back
where the Victorians began, with hourly deliveries
and even less to say. Eden was a version of the subtropics

in which we knew what was forbidden: unshaven hair
furred your inner thighs, the afternoon you explained,
in languorous detail, why you could never love me.

Not an exit line but an exit wound.

x. Jews

Jews founded their banks with a taste for conspiracy.
Even the papers keep kosher in discontent,
or so the brutal choose to believe, these summers

of bombs, judicial murder, *Kristallnacht* every night.
How efficient the Germans, the death factories,
as if death too were catchy merchandise, its corporations

listed on the Bourse or Wall Street. (How many
trays of soap, gold teeth addressed to safe-deposit boxes?)
How long did memory steel itself to new murder,

Stalin galloping down the peasants, Mao's
common graves, Pol Pot's killing fields,
East Timor, Rwanda, the history-dark Balkans?

The names blur, minor holocausts drifting away.
What Goya saw in the etcher's needle goes on
being seen. Death dines with a reservation,

never too hungry, knowing his next meal will come:
the ash of ash, the dust of unwilling dust.
Years after the war, the towns had lost their synagogues.

No one living remembered where they had been.

xi. The Real Thing

Kill the houselights and the unconscious confesses,
or so it remains in London theater. I sleep
through second acts, after the first warms the blood

to the steam-heat anarchy of dream. In the public dark,
the actors delivered a play within the play,
stage mock affairs or, who knows, real ones.

This was called a revival. In the first run, the playwright
cast a blonde as the obscure wife of the playwright,
each prefix mimicking the hazard of conversation,

or what we, passive observers lit up in the lazy
ambient glow of the spots, heard as the privileged echo.
Was she naked each night beneath the blue bathrobe,

as she flashed his neglectful alter ego?
Are there lives not humiliated in their second acts?
Soon after, or long enough, he left his wife for her,

another reason, you say, never to get married.
You took the interval standing in line for the toilet,
and reported the stalls so tiny no one shut the doors.

A metaphor for the private life, perhaps.

xii. Garbo

Like Garbo you took to your room, a headache
coming on, but yours lasted months, years.
Ordinary life went on around you, on the sidewalk

six feet from your blinded windows. You ordered in.
New York promises hot blood when you're young;
at fifty it's the half-lit world you know, rent-controlled,

life in installments, pleasure cast-iron or crumbling.
No one believes in Freud when the antidepressants kick in—
the new therapy is an alarm clock of Elavil or Prozac.

Who hasn't felt his forties a fast-forward film?
On the mapled campus, we were still appealingly young
when you slit open proofs of my studio photographs,

trying to find a way to bewilder yourself into love.
In minutes they faded in the forgiving sun, my faces bland
and pale as pastry. One night I huddled in my car and wept,

wept for years, and woke up cured. Seeing you
in a Manhattan restaurant, the second time
this decade, I hardly recognized who you were.

Then that sly smile, and I felt myself falling again.

xiii. Maple Leaves

Maple leaves spurring off the branch in clusters,
overlapping like wing feathers, piled up, cross-turned,
spill down summer's page like Japanese brushwork,

or a Fifth Avenue hat in the divided forties.
Half a decade lost to war, half to recovery,
the heady nights of the GI Bill and victory sidecars.

The leaves remember, remember the sergeant uncle
who shipped home porcelain from occupied Japan,
a Napoleon wheeling away Venice's bronze horses.

And then the breeze rises and the vision shudders:
the secular is toying with the eternal, now.
Each crimson stem snagging dawn like a cut vein,

the shadows of Spanish moss stir the dirt
for the fragrance of the soul. We are responsible
to the sins that gave birth to us. Augustine grass

half-carpets our dry tropical seabed. The developer
has half-finished his limestone wall—ragged, pierced
memory of the field walls of glacial New England,

remembering partly to forgive, partly to forget.

xiv. Austen

No, Miss Dashwood. I do declare, Miss Dashwood!
In the cold shires of Jane-ites, rough scones slouching
across Laura Ashley tablecloths, the clotted creams seduce

the pots of strawberry jam. Wet-eared PhDs manhandle her
for ignoring the bull market of scholarship.
This year she approves of slavery—

the evidence, as they say, in the absence.
An owl-eyed Home Secretary proposes to throw into prison
the criminal before the crime—*Capital Sense,*

the Queen of Hearts might roar. Who would be immune?
No author is innocent of the spoil of ink.
Justice kneels to the smear of DNA,

stained with sins before they've begun to sin,
unless we believe in the Virgin Birth, a tale
even vicars find hard to swallow. Like most utopias,

the new world cancels its passport to the old,
where a witty phrase could win you a pension
or unite in marriage Sensibility and Sense,

two old families now down on their luck.

xv. Endurance

Once upon a time, began the old tale,
and that's how we knew it was a tale. Shackleton's
fare-thee-well voyage, ship marooned in ice,

crew booting a soccer ball across the shelf,
the photographer tilting his flash pots to catch
hoarfrost in the rigging. I splay my fingers

over their mute images, a century later,
knowing their fate as they could not, as others
will know our fates, though we cannot. The hull cracked

like matchsticks. Mere tragicomedy, unlike Franklin
starving with his crew, Hudson and his boy adrift.
The men of the *Endurance,* crossing at the worst season,

low on provision, made landfall at a forgotten
whaling station, Shackleton pressing on,
the stumpy ketch a scar in crosshatched sea,

the captain's sun-sighting through muffled cloud
a feat of reckoning judged greater than Bligh's.
And still an ice mountain to traverse with frayed rope,

the heroism not presence of virtue, or absence of vanity.

xvi. Coup de grâce

Pity the uses of obscurity. Each word dangles
the promiscuity of rich misuse, like an earring.
On hands and knees, beneath the couch

where we'd made love, you scrabbled in frustration,
naked, ass in the air, revealing those passive graces
submission desires. Despite the ambiguity

of all you say, or cannot say,
we live in an age of reasons, never reason,
the blessed Virgin a vision in a pancake in one city,

a water stain in a small town, as if flour or plaster
were soiled with *fin de siècle* immanence
as the millennium drains from the clawfoot tub.

Forgive the sins of our departing century.
Where Othello mistook the handkerchief for a sign,
it led to a death, to death and further death.

We live in sign and wonder, juddering headlights
mistaken for UFOs. *It's not personal,*
they said as the Luger nuzzled her ear,

as if there were no signs or wonders left.

xvii. Small Town

Quite early, there was something to answer for,
the two-room schoolhouse boiled in the dusty yard,
the broken backs of saltbox houses, staggering

beneath the overhang of the Baltimore oriole.
The starboard facade of the Methodist church
fronted the common cemetery, burnished lichen

and stitched stone, teaching the corpus of Christian love.
Not a word was spoken, though we were tiny
incarnations of the Word, with our Sunday-school badges

of good attendance. Each sermon grabbled the air,
there in the long aftermath of Peter's charity,
Paul's prejudicial letters, a church founded

(allegedly) by fishermen. In our deviant sect,
one more heresy moved the fractured service,
while local tuna-men netted the Pope's encyclicals:

fish on Friday, and grace the rest of the week.
Suspended beyond the charms of a world
that buried its dead and kept silence,

we were left to discover the *Zeitgeist* for ourselves.

xviii. Alphabet

Ratio, ration, peroration. Martyr to choice
and the fealty of memory, the student of these lessons
that have never intended easy answers.

Aluminum is to Ayer as bread is to brainpan.
Clam is to *corrigenda* as drum kit to Descartes.
Erasmus is to Eveready as frankincense to foghorn.

Ghost is to Grand Canal as Hegel to harm's way,
Intimacy is to ideal as James to jury duty.
Kill switch is to Krakatoa as lighthouse to Locke.

Mill is to measles as neurosis to Nietzsche.
Opera is to Ockham as pumpkin to parallelogram.
Quiescence is to quilt as Rousseau to retrograde amnesia.

Sartre is to silicon as trinity to tergiversation.
Underwear is to U-boat as Vico to vanity.
Waterpower is to Wittgenstein as Xerox to X-ray.

Yellow fever is to yearning as Zeno to zero.
In the layers of the ABC's, further incantation and error.
The first cause was innocence, then came

lines of poetry like falling ranks. Onward!

xix. Coleridge

Saddled with debt, he saddled himself to dragoons,
under the *nom de guerre* of Comberbache, Silas T.
Better to ride against French hussars than the brute

alexandrines of Racine. The American war was over,
red jackets soaking the ground at Yorktown.
In Cambridge it was easier to catch shingles

than learning, there in the dissolute abbey, rebuilt
along a ditch of moorhens and thorned chestnuts.
Through unheated rooms plied with the merchants'

dunning copperplate, rough winds whistled the fens.
America, your new found land! To pluck
from the gazetteer the Susquehanna and plot a family,

a pantisocracy, which sounds like government by clothing
or another method of escaping musty, moleskin England.
The problem of tailoring began with Schiller.

All that to the future, and now only the drilling,
the interminable smell, horseflesh and men flesh.
1798: *I have snapped my squeaking baby trumpet of Sedition*

& the fragments lie scattered in the lumber-room of Penitence.

xx. Therapy

Two centuries lost (count the lost wars), plumes
on horseback, enough for the dress trade:
looking back never measures the gaze into the blank

mist of the still-to-come. What is to come?
Seers, haruspices, glass-ball gypsies, palm-readers,
newspaper horoscopists, psychics, Ouija board players,

weather forecasters, penny-stock speculators, priests.
Every sibyl a sectarian, each oracle a tout:
what is to come has already come again:

wheat fields impotent in drought, rivers walking
across Asia, seaweed smothering the Mediterranean.
The Romantics would salve the conscience in therapy—

who can imagine Coleridge on the couch, tyrant
of the talking cure? What a boon for the private life:
each tin-pot demiurge arms himself,

squeaking on the radio, pleading to be understood.
Thus we keep banker's hours. Thus dawn,
spattered with English cloud, lifts the slate housetops.

Squadrons of chimney swifts sweep the chill air.

xxi. The Weather

Under the weather, meaning the flesh
no longer tolerates the possibility of loss
even in loss, like Hector when he knew

his bronze armor would be dragged through the dust.
Even at spear-point, he did not want to be Achilles,
twice-drowned, under sentence and waiting to die.

My forties rehearsed the deathwatch, parents
withering like overripe plums, old lovers succumbing
to a compound death no different from a stranger's,

except they were flesh in my flesh. I wandered
through the vandalized graveyard, stones
snapped at the base, names rubbed raw by weather

(a few decades and we are unwritten), old tombs
flung open, the marble tilted like sinking rafts.
Elsewhere, men buried their dead above ground,

giving the corpse an even chance against high water,
the hurricane tide of . . . palimpsest, erasure,
the future that couldn't pronounce our names

if it knew them, and it will not know them.

xxii. Venice

Venice, old city of dreams underwater,
arms rising to the surface, oily, rippled,
never reached. The ceiling above our bed

opened to cloudscape, fresco of the gods
engaged in godlike, amused work
(requiring some mortal's rape or murder)

by a minor follower of a minor follower of Tiepolo.
Outside, like souls, lizards scattered over roof tiles.
The city of the future will be drowned;

each year it sinks a fraction lower into debt.
We return like shallow ghosts to our old walks,
as if to see again were to make the past visible.

Déjà vu. My old theory: no shop ever vanishes—
around a corner on dusty shelves lie the lost plays
of Sophocles, or Shakespeare's *Love's Labours Wonne.*

We breathe the dust of a past we soon become.
We rescue from the past what it can afford,
as Europe borrowed from the canals of Venice,

as Venice stole from the warrens of Byzantium.

xxiii. **Wren**

Wren raised his masterpiece on what the wreckers left,
as if the incendiaries had fallen on Venice,
where baroque classicism had its knees in water.

Along the sewers Londoners used as a canal,
the cobbles became convinced of their destiny.
The Great Fire reduced itself to a great fire.

The herring have been sluiced from Billingsgate
and raddled sheep have defected from Haymarket.
Though ships carry disease from the ports

and rats demand union wages and paid holidays,
the ancient pub still serves raw beef like a wound.
The Roman walls offer no moral protection from the IRA.

Nothing compares to loneliness, half a century gone,
a quarter-century, more or less, to get through.
In the green belt, a gray scrim hangs behind butchered trees,

under a sky dashed off for stage-set England.
Moore's altar sits like a chicken vertebra
in the middle of St. Stephen Walbrook.

The rose of fire crosses the trellis of a bombed city.

xxiv. Byzantium (Interlude)

X-ray. Dome welded to dome like spheres of heaven,
Sinan's Sulimaniye mosque, a pail of gilt mushroom caps.
Leadwork intricate as pierced marble ripples the brow

of the most serene of the seven hills. Think
how it looked, minarets pointed like spindles,
tracery carved like a legal document for the unwashed,

unshriven ambassadors, born to Peter's cathedral,
strutting under the painted sailcloth of a ship
drawn up the Bosphorus to the guttural Horn,

sails of a dozen geometries, the faith of rigging—
not just Byzantine cathedrals defaced,
but faith glaring against the hills, world born to perfection

remade in sin, whose golden birds whispered in the dirt.
Where were they, the matte portions of our lives?
Another world was written into the lines of your face.

I expected to age, not to get any older,
to age into perfection; and then one July morning
a stranger lived in the mirror, not unfriendly,

just a man who could never inhabit the past.

xxv. Nature

You know how love divides its proper spoils.
I hardly dare look you in the eye, since you
if anyone know how readily the lie

trespasses the tongue, how simple to suffer
in silence what is more convenient to praise.
Time is condemned to go in circles on the watch,

but does not punish so much as refuse to answer.
Pity the future, black canvas stretched taut,
awaiting the unknown. Much easier

to look back, as if the past were familiar,
though often as not we have lost its address.
Houses stand vacant where we knew

a few minutes of happiness or self-love.
Friends who have caught the last train
to whatever destination lies below the horizon

still inhabit our predicate, unlovely city,
perhaps a little aside their old apartments.
We hear their familiar greetings with the consolation

of what Nature offers, struck dumb in error.

xxvi. *The River*

Zero hour. The streets cooling in aftermath,
papers offer news new-risen each morning.
Agents unlock their shops to fresh loaves

cheaper than newsprint and without headlines.
The river lies like a blank mirror. *The Mirror.*
The Sun. Along the common, dark-stippled with dew,

no swans break the burnished, unconscious water.
Their ancestors breasted the sluggish stream
proudly, as befitted feathered property of a queen.

Local constables have been dragging the depths.
Gaffhooked bikes lie on the bank like corpses.
The weedy Cerberus squats—a fax machine hauled

from the reeds. Everywhere riverboats
have moored illicitly, a patched, doleful city afloat.
And then, as the old gasworks rises into sight,

a kingfisher darts upriver, metallic blue,
a crossbow bolt soon lost to the willows.
O Daily Telegraph. O Daily Mail. O The Times.

Give us a sign. We would have a wonder and a sign.

MISS LONELYHEARTS

The Mexican Revolution drew you in
like a Venus flytrap—
not Díaz but the yapping Marxists.
The Embassy refused to bail you out,

morbid, moon-eyed American
fallen from suntan to prison pallor
in a month of Sundays,
each morning tin trinkets of the Church,

and every afternoon, siesta.
Months later you crossed the campus
like a deer harried by dogs.
Your office had barred windows.

That late northern winter,
the snow was like chicken fat,
the flocks were dyed beet-red for slaughter.
Students found excuse

to linger for advice, Miss Lonelyhearts,
after your course in *Das Kapital*.
Who could have predicted the spring's vastation?
Your shrine to Keats,

the corner of foolscap broken
from the Widener ms. of "The Eve of St. Agnes,"
was swept up by some janitor.
You survived the short sentence of marriage

on French éclairs and the *New York Times*.
Did neither of us wish to face
the uncertain lines of a future, any future?
The vanity table's

thin, cracked, unforgiving mirror
mocked my blue felt-tip's cocksure corrections.
You said: *Every ideology is finally theology—*
I mean, it starts as fertilizer and ends as manure.

THE DEVIL'S TOENAIL

A SEASHELL

What might enshrine
geology's raw nerve
or a French curve
spiraling through the line

edging this broken shape,
this porous, paid-for lime,
endowed the rugged climb
down the stone landscape

into a present marked
by sediment's raw fear,
laid down year by year,
each grain a miniature ark.

Curved as a coracle,
the fossil shell stood out
amid the gravel rout
like the bone of an oracle,

waiting for the words
to make the future sense
as Romans at some expense
did from the livers of birds.

Do two lovers owe
the strangers they were at the start
more than their faltering hearts?
The past would say no.

ODALISQUE

And so she took off her shirt, all
in one motion, making her brief
hesitation an act of modesty,
yet immodest. We had not had

an affair, and could never have an affair.
It was not that she was not beautiful,
though she wasn't, and not that I
didn't know the desire of other men

to sleep with her. The Atlantic
lay in the harbor, fusing its blue disorders
to the light slatted through blinds,
the light that barred her breasts.

They were, need I say, nearly perfect.
I saw how proud she was of them,
proud too of their effect on men,
and I knew I wasn't the first man

before whom, in one sinuous motion,
she had stripped off her shirt.
It made her vulnerable, that mute beauty,
thinking no man who saw her naked

could control his desire. Even after
I had refused her, she had been unable to stop.
She looked away, as if in shyness,
to let me watch her as she wanted to be watched.

Then she put on her other shirt.
When I saw her recently, twenty years
had passed, and those years cruel
to women, even women you love.

ACHILLES

Down into the folly, you took my hand.
Red moon under the scudding cloud,
the sheep bearing their gray, thorned realm

past the thistle and the ruined elm,
and all silent, silent as cloth.
We had taken the rock-guarded path

along a horizon shaken on the west wind.
Below us, the land spread out
toward an old hall lit by candles

against the sparking wood. Somewhere,
the clink of a chain
and the dim almost rustle of evening.

The cracked mirror
of Capability's lake turned livid, glinting
like a flutter of moths. Then we stepped down

onto the field of ghostly cattle
moving their great horned helmets against us.
The air was antique with breath.

And there stood Achilles, the famous bull,
proudly aside from the herd,
massive, scarred, nursing his anger.

He turned toward us in his naked heat.

CRANE AMONG THE COMMONERS

England, then. The house of duchesses,
the pocket boroughs cramped with pale MPs,
and fistfuls of extraordinary crackers.
How catch, where his new-fangled prose would fail
the dry emulsions of a photograph,
the London *bonne femme* under buffalo robes?

Such cities sat upon the mantel, now.
Civilization stained the emptiness
unseen, each feather-duster tumbleweed,
each river crooked as a signature.
He'd seen men buckshot, drowned, longing to die,
but death remained a whirligig of fate,

its pinned arms flailing at the inevitable.
The sick know justice as a troubled dream:
debt always at the door like a pet dog,
champagne on ice, and lunch on truffled pheasant,
the good life only good if bought and paid
in constant damp, inconstant friends, new pages

scrolled down the platen like a prairie storm.
So much a page, borrowed against the past,
the past he thinned to filmy onionskin,
twirling the Smith & Wesson at his desk.
There was a dream within the dream, a dream
where Henry James ate a doughnut in the garden,

where Yankee girls named Praline, Orange, and Sunset
promised a heartsore mildness, whose residence
had oddly left no forwarding address.

BANK VOLES AT TRINITY COLLEGE, CAMBRIDGE

At first the damp leaves
rustled with the thought
of unharvested sheaves
and undergrads untaught,

the myrtle greens, the browns
of soggy paper bags
or satin May Ball gowns
with designer tags.

Startled like a fear,
the stubby, red-haired mouse
showed its tufted rear
above a weed-choked house,

taking a nervous pause
beneath the shadowy leaf,
unworried by the cause
of rage, despair, or grief,

or sins that separate
man from a mouse so wary,
our rough but certain fate
in Eden's bestiary.

Through the star-crossed town,
each bottle of champagne
escorted a brilliant gown
down a college lane.

Love places us in a line
stretching back to the fish
that left the ocean brine
for the land's gibberish,

but no man comprehends
the reason of his birth,
or that he'll lie in the end
beneath the weedy earth,

where the common vole,
a sacrificial pawn,
intends to be small but whole
some generations on.

THE WAX-MODELERS

To make wax models of the dead,
    their livers, lungs, and broken hearts,
    is not the lowliest of arts.
The feelings must be cast in lead.

Where does the mortal soul exist?
    In dry apartments of a fate
    where noisy unpaid Shylocks wait
the resurrection of the dead.

In heaven will our bodies take
    the form they loved themselves to be
    in some austere philosophy
that kept our living selves awake?

Or will the naked dead surround
    us at the cold gates of the gods,
    who claim that though we beat the odds
we lost our beauty underground?

Pity the dead in their distress:
    Rochefoucauld knew, or should have known,
    we meet our long decay alone.
True love, like prayer, is pitiless.

The brighter clothing of our flesh
    will drop away, and leave its mark
    in all that genuflective dark
where we must learn to sin afresh.

IN THE MUSEUM

THE FAYUM MUMMY PORTRAITS

Graeco-Egyptians, Ptolemy's distant sons,
inherited the land, a coinage, and an attitude.
Dark-eyed, long-nosed, half-Asian, half-European,
they can't stay dead, rising from the sand
like new-fledged falcons to the startled light,
shocked by how easy it was to die.
In flaking emerald and corrupted pearl,
the torpor of millennia underground
tears at their ball-gown tunics and half-smiles,
faces that found their language invisible—
the secret of their afterlife was, no afterlife.

AFTER EASTER

The skylight filled with snow, like whitened ash.
Three traders flagged a taxi going south.
Inside the bank, the ATM spat cash—
you put your shivering fingers in its mouth.

Knowing tomorrow's temperature would rise,
Manhattan churned the Easter snow to mud.
I saw the faintest passion in your eyes.
The doctors found new cancer in your blood.

There is a pocket war in Mexico.
Those years when you were dangerous to know—
Where did they come from? Would they never go?
The tech stocks made another leap; the Dow Jones soared.
If love remains, what's left of love is snow:
out in the street, the choking gutters roared.

ADULTERY

Cars broke past the park and throttled home,
foreign, unhealthy, collegial,
their groaning the groaning of the sea.
What is it good for, identity?

Common as fingerprints, our lives
burn like decaying atoms
across the dark cloud of the negative.
And there on the mantel your wedding photo,

two people fresh and immortal as Saran Wrap!
Your skin had a godlike sheen.
Children, mortgages, the blurred fangs of dogs,
how easily the stopwatch halts

at five years, at twenty.
You stare past the mirror and no one
has your father's grizzled face,
that nasty new simmer of a smile,

a lover and daughter and a new address.
You saunter out to feed the parking meter,
as if, each dawn, time were starting over
again, and then again, and again,

as if paying for life is all there is to life.
We've been traded in, says your angry wife.

LYING IN BED

I can't take back the lies I gave to you,
the day-by-days we chose to live apart,
and one more lie will never make them true.

Chain saws have canceled elms along the avenue.
The change in government is now a chart.
I can't take back the lies I gave to you,

but, even if I could, they'd be a clue
that gave our brand-new lies a place to start.
One more lie will never make them true.

Trust is a poison, the fatal residue
in small cafés that serve lies à la carte.
I can't take back the lies I gave to you.

For me it was the lies that made love new.
For me it was the lies that made love art,
but one more lie will never make them true.

What is truth anyway, but overdue
lies whose late arrival breaks your heart?
I can't take back the lies I gave to you,
and one more lie will never make them true.

SONG

The years have been cruel, dear, the years have been cruel.
They kick like a mule, dear, they kick like a mule.

The years have been cruel, dear, the years have been cruel.
O that is the rule, dear, that is the rule.

The years have been cruel, dear, the years have been cruel.
They use us for fuel, dear, they use us for fuel.

The years will be kind, dear, the years will be kind.
O pay them no mind, dear, pay them no mind.

SEVEN DEADLY SIN

There's the sin of where's the money,
the sin of you love me too much,
the sin of something's missing,
the sin of please don't touch.

There's the sin of it meant nothing,
the sin of please don't go,
the sin of don't come back here
with the sin of you'll never know.

There's the sin of I'll never leave you,
the sin of you don't care,
the sin of you can trust me,
but I have to do my hair.

There's the sin of I never loved you,
and the sin where north meets south
and the sin of please have my baby
and I won't come in your mouth.

There's seven deadly sin, my love,
seven deadly sin,
and it's never a sin if you do them all
with a little discipline.

EPITAPH ON AN EDITOR

Rejection, of a kind, was what he was after,
and the poetry he published was easy to understand;
he thought a poem should be like the back of his hand,
and never more complicated than barley or beets;
When he laughed, minor poets applauded his disasters,
and when he died little elegies were hung in the streets.

TRANSLATION

You bought a car with a dodgy transmission
and tooled around looking for trouble,
always in second gear. Bad wiring
left a rear window lowered, as if winking.

Mostly you drove the gravel driveway,
where the *woppa-woppa* of a woodpecker,
beating its head against the clapboard
like a pile driver, echoed like a magnum at close quarters—

even the effort wasn't worth the effort.
Champagne, or a .357?
The leaf-fall ricochet of dried-up magnolias
died in slow motion, though Galileo

might have disagreed—huge, waxy, razor-edged,
the leaves fell, lazy as a guillotine,
full of morals and indifference.
In the sand that pretended to be soil,

grass had a toehold, but no commitments.
Someone might have excavated
a collapsed temple of Mithras,
had this been Rome. His believers

worshiped the mystery of the bull,
and gave the Christians a run for their money.
Our lawn took on a sickly, yellowish haze,
one of the problems of translation.

PRAYER

ON A SCULPTURE BY GEORG KOLBE

The spirit of the rough air, cast in bronze,
kneels naked on the gallery's wooden floor,
a fallen girl of fallen Babylons,
a primitive insect trapped in amber ore.

Like Eve, each woman tastes a man's desire
more by the reputation of the tongue
and chooses for herself what men require,
no matter how indifferent, or young.

Love left a trace in its apocrypha.
Like Eve before her, she was born to please.
Now taking off her panties and her bra,
she opens her mouth, and then goes down on her knees.

THE RUINS OF OSTIA ANTICA

The grasses wavered on the autumn light,
   their seedy heads toppled with beaten gold,
a warning to the shy, corrupted town:

   there the fields were browsed like a gnawn scalp,
the cattle wretched and malevolent.
   Their dry coughs startled the staring, curious rooks,

   which perched like mournful groups of murderers
among the stinging nettles. Creatures, creatures!
   How lavish the settlement upon the meek,

how lush the hot breath raking their dry necks.
   They stand in the ruins of the architect,
the butted stone, the scatter of quiet mosaic—

   the fish contrived from squares of blackened glass,
the speckled ships sailing on waves of stone,
   the disembodied stare of the hunted god.

They wait for something less than martyrdom,
   stooping to crop the heresies of grass
beneath a broken doorway of the sun.

ON THE ACQUISITION OF
PLEASURE IN SMALL GROUPS

i. Spas

How each cool evening chilled the water doctors
driving their landaus past historic spas,
the solfège of the oaks lashing across

the ruined scale of Adam and Palladio.
Carpets roll out again like woolen tongues;
the dusty band strikes up a martial air,

each diagnosis Greek in treatment and effect.
To contravene the lady with her dog,
their rudimentary knowledge of anatomy

takes the dumb liver for the beating heart.
By deft appointment to a prince, cool nymphs
bearing the rotted eggs at Harrogate

cure barrenness and eyesight at a glance.
How savor the crawling beetle or the worm?
We vary in our gift for punishment,

fallible God who tests our wavering faith
with falling waters, sprays, and cataracts
wrapped in wet sheets, the Old Gout Road's unease.

So Jesus chose the cure at Calvary,
where from his side poured holy vinegars—
to drown, to save a dry land's politics.

ii. Pleasure Gardens

To own a pleasure garden served the just
necessity, written against the stars.
In oil-lamp London, stars winked out at night,

building by building down the grass-laid malls,
each cold fog rising like a spectral saint
who laid his martyrdom in Butler's *Saints*,

the life a grotto overcome with worship.
Their agues argue nightly, mephitic gases
oozing with coffee-house cosmology

as dogs lap rumors of the other world.
Here a grand wooden lion frowns like stone,
the alehouse turns an intimate affair

to public gaze, the longing solitude
crowds porticoes, rotundas, colonnades
(each overgrown with ivies, star-shaped lamps),

gloomy pale lawns, the mildewed dripping vaults,
bowers, pavilions, lodges, chapels, groves.
Refine our salty pleasures, Old Refinement.

Religion's sanction of a sanctified despair
gilds the brash garden gates like gates of heaven.
The rite of spring befouls *The Rights of Man*.

iii. The Death of Kings

The shape of kingdoms shares the death of kings,
the river curling to the sovereign mass
where lagging flocks, touched with the waterbrain,

crawl home. Night comes, damp with old satisfaction,
its rarified, down-at-heels, pinched scholar's glare,
knowing, unknowing, all pages inked alike

in mock defiance of authority,
the taste of God for kings, or kings for men.
In twenty years, a hundred, who recalls

the blotted love, the chiseled name effaced?
Gravediggers laugh, the new officials mourn,
then turn to stately pleasures once again—

repression stiffens into chivalry.
Remember that the memory has failed,
that slowing breezes cure the ravens' stare

as winter ices shut the muted pond.
Tourists will loll in peeling boats at dusk,
as if the painter who composed the scene

raised some extinct museum of the past,
where murdered kings left fossil memories
new kingdoms would be forced to memorize.

THE ROMAN VILLA

SOCINIANISM MOONLIGHT—METHODISM A STOVE!
                                    Coleridge, *Notebooks*

Religion in the late light
crosses the ploughed field.
A startled hare winces
on the moon's struck shield:

the turf pulled back like a skin,
the sorrel disarrayed
on the dressed stone.
Frayed grasses gleam like jade:

resurrection writhes the shallow trench.
Naked, the dirt and underdirt.
The villa lines its kept grave
with rye and liverwort,

the passage over the Styx
paid with the empire's coin,
black tesserae, shattered hypocaust,
the dead mason's quoin.

This, all this postscript,
the new sun chiefly gilt,
a drenched, ungrateful particular,
the word sunk to the hilt.

THE OLD BURYING GROUND

March's bitter morning thawed
　　the frozen skin of the Sound
as Harvard's Gothic shadow fell
　　upon the burying ground.

Snow in its gelid costume dressed
　　the icy stand of birch
where the tilted gravestones shelved
　　against the First Parish church.

The leafless birches sank within
　　the shallow swamp of snow,
a Japanese rice-paper screen's
　　calligraphy aglow,

like great blue herons stalking
　　carp in silent pools
beneath the melting icicles'
　　glassy, dripping jewels.

The birches formed their rank above
　　the waters of Paradise,
warming the gravestones' chiseled names
　　in Dante's lake of ice.

On standing pools wind shivered
　　over the traitorous dead,
where starving Ugolino gnawed
　　Archbishop Roger's head.

The winter's sculptured rites of snow,
     like glittering evidence,
looked forward to the crocuses
     teasing the iron fence,

the mourners each spring resurrected
     to words no longer said;
but memory of the dead will never
     resurrect the dead.

The promises the living swear
     betray their long decrease—
the mourner's lie In Memory Of,
     the fraud of Rest in Peace,

where buried on this sacred ground,
     in frozen, barren earth,
lie the distant soiled past
     and frenzied rage of birth.

NOTE

"An Englishwoman in America" is based on passages in Barbara Leigh Smith Bodichon's *An American Diary 1857–8* (London, 1972).

PENGUIN POETS